Who
Is Jesus?

C000000168

Booklets taken from Questions of Life:

Is There More to Life Than This?

Who Is Jesus?

Why Did Jesus Die?

How Can We Have Faith?

Why and How Do I Pray?

Why and How Should I Read the Bible?

How Does God Guide Us?

The Holy Spirit

How Can I Resist Evil?

Why and How Should I Tell Others?

Does God Heal Today?

What About the Church?

How Can I Make the Most of the Rest of My Life?

Who
Is Jesus?

NICKY GUMBEL

Scripture quotations taken from
the Holy Bible, New International
Version Anglicised. Copyright ©
1979, 1984, 2011 Biblica, formerly
International Bible Society. Used by
permission of Hodder & Stoughton
Publishers, an Hachette UK
company. All rights reserved. 'NIV'
is a registered trademark of Biblica.
UK trademark number 1448790.

Published by Alpha International
Holy Trinity Brompton
Brompton Road
London SW7 1JA
Email: publications@alpha.org

Illustrated by Charlie Mackesy

Contents

Who Is Jesus?

For much of my life I was not interested in Christianity. My father was a secular Jew and my mother rarely went to church. I was at times an atheist and at times an agnostic, unsure of what I believed. I had studied the Bible in religion classes at school, but had ended up rejecting it all and arguing against the Christian faith. On Valentine's Night 1974, my convictions were challenged by my closest friend Nicky Lee. I had just returned from a party when Nicky and his girlfriend appeared and told me that they had just become Christians. I was horrified! I had come across Christians during the year that I had taken off between school and university and I was deeply suspicious of them, in particular their tendency to smile so much.

I knew I had to help my friends, so I thought that I would embark on some thorough research of the subject. I happened to have a rather dusty copy of the Bible on my shelves, so that night I picked it up and started reading. I read all the way through Matthew,

Mark and Luke, and halfway through John's Gospel. I fell asleep. When I woke up, I finished John's Gospel and carried on through Acts, Romans, and 1 and 2 Corinthians. I was completely gripped by what I read. Previously it had meant virtually nothing to me. This time it came alive and I could not put it down. It had a ring of truth about it. I knew as I read it I had to respond because it spoke so powerfully to me. Very shortly afterwards I put my faith in Jesus Christ.

However, later I spent nearly ten years studying law and practising as a barrister – so for me evidence is very important. I could not have taken a blind leap of faith, but was willing to take a step of faith based on good historical evidence. In this booklet I want to examine some of this historical evidence.

I am told that in an old communist Russian dictionary Jesus is described as 'a mythical figure who never existed'. No serious historian would maintain that position today. There is a great deal of evidence for Jesus' existence. This comes not only from the Gospels and other Christian writings, but also from other sources. For example, the Roman historians Tacitus and Suetonius both wrote about him. The Jewish historian Josephus, born in AD 37, describes Jesus and his followers thus:

> Now there was about this time, Jesus, a wise man, if it be lawful to call him a man, for he was a doer of wonderful works – a teacher of such men as receive the truth with pleasure. He drew over to him both many of the Jews, and many of the Gentiles.[1]

So there is evidence outside the New Testament for the existence of Jesus. Furthermore, the evidence in the New Testament is very strong. Sometimes people say, 'The New Testament was written a long time ago. How do we know that what they wrote down has not been changed over the years?' The answer is that we do know, very accurately, through the science of textual criticism, what the New Testament writers wrote. Essentially, the shorter the time span between the date the manuscript was written and the earliest available copy, the more texts we have, and the higher the quality of the existing texts, the less doubt there is about the original.

The late Professor F. F. Bruce (who was Rylands Professor of Biblical Criticism and Exegesis at the University of Manchester) shows in his book, *The New Testament Documents: Are They Reliable?* how wealthy the New Testament is in manuscript attestation by comparing its texts with other historical works.[2] The table overleaf summarises the facts and shows the extent of the evidence for the New Testament's authenticity.

Work	When Written	Earliest copy	Time span (years)	No. of copies
Herodotus	488–428 BC	AD 900	1,300	8
Thucydides	c. 460–400 BC	c. AD 900	1,300	8
Tacitus	AD 100	1100	1,000	20
Caesar's Gallic Wars	58–50 BC	AD 900	950	9–10
Livy's Roman History	59 BC – AD 17	AD 900	900	20
New Testament	AD 40–100	AD 130 (full manuscripts AD 350)	300	5,000+ Greek 10,000 Latin 9,300 others

F. F. Bruce points out that for Caesar's *Gallic War* we have nine or ten copies and the oldest was written some 950 years later than Caesar's day. For Livy's *History of Rome* we have not more than twenty copies, the earliest of which comes from around AD 900, though none of these are complete. Of the fourteen books of Tacitus' *Histories* only twenty copies survive; of the surviving sixteen books of his *Annals*, ten portions of his two great historical works depend entirely on two manuscripts, one of the ninth century and one of the eleventh century. The history of Thucydides is known almost entirely from eight manuscripts belonging to c. AD 900. The same is true of Herodotus' *Histories*. Yet no classical scholar doubts the authenticity of these works, in spite of the large time gap and the relatively small number of manuscripts.

As regards the New Testament, we have a great abundance of material. The New Testament was probably written between AD 40 and AD 100. We have excellent full manuscripts for the whole New Testament dating from as early as AD 350 (a time span of only 300 years), papyri containing most of the New Testament writings dating from the third century and even a fragment of John's Gospel, which scientists have carbon-dated to around AD 125. There are over 5,000 Greek manuscripts, over 10,000 Latin manuscripts and 9,300 other manuscripts, together with more than 36,000 citations in the writings of the early church fathers. As one of the greatest ever textual critics, F. J. A. Hort, said, 'In the variety and fullness of the evidence on which it rests, the text of the New Testament stands absolutely and unapproachably alone among ancient prose writings.'[3]

F. F. Bruce summarises the evidence by quoting Sir Frederic Kenyon, a leading scholar in this area:

> The interval then between the dates of original composition and the earliest extant evidence

> becomes so small as to be in fact negligible,
> and the last foundation for any doubt that the
> Scriptures have come down to us substantially
> as they were written has now been removed.
> Both the *authenticity* and the *general integrity*
> of the books of the New Testament may be
> regarded as finally established.[4]

We know then from different types of evidence both outside and inside the New Testament that Jesus existed.[5] But who is he? I heard Martin Scorsese say on television that he made the film *The Last Temptation of Christ* in order to show that Jesus was a real human being. Yet that is not the issue at the moment. Few people today would doubt that Jesus was fully human. He had a human body; he was sometimes tired (John 4:6) and hungry (Matthew 4:2). He had human emotions; he was angry (Mark 11:15–17), he loved (Mark 10:21) and he was sad (John 11:35). He had human experiences: he grew up in a family (Mark 6:3), he had a job (Mark 6:3), he was tempted (Mark 1:13) and he experienced suffering and death (Mark 15:15–40).

What many say today is that Jesus was *only* a human being – albeit a great religious teacher. The comedian Billy Connolly spoke for many when he said, 'I can't believe in Christianity, but I think Jesus was a wonderful man.' What evidence is there to suggest that Jesus was more than just a man of staggering influence or a great moral teacher? The answer, as we shall see, is that there is a great deal of evidence. This evidence supports the Christian contention that Jesus was, and is, the unique Son of God, the second person of the Trinity.

What did he say about himself?

Some people say, 'Jesus never claimed to be God.' Indeed, it is true that Jesus did not go around saying the words, 'I am God.' Yet when one looks at all he taught and claimed, there is little doubt that he was conscious of being a person whose identity was God.

Teaching centred on himself

One of the fascinating things about Jesus is that so much of his teaching was centred on himself. Most religious leaders point away from themselves and to God, as we would expect. Jesus, the most humble and self-effacing person who ever lived, in pointing people to God, pointed to himself. He said, in effect, 'If you want to have a relationship with God, you need to come to me' (John 14:6). It is through a relationship with him that we encounter God.

There is a hunger deep within the human heart. Three leading psychologists of the twentieth century have all recognised this. Freud said, 'People are hungry for love.' Jung said, 'People are hungry for security.'

Adler said, 'People are hungry for significance.' Jesus said, 'I am the bread of life' (John 6:35). In other words, 'If you want your hunger satisfied, come to me.'

Addiction is a major problem in our society. Speaking about himself, Jesus said, 'If the Son sets you free, you will be free indeed' (John 8:36).

Many people are depressed, disillusioned and in a dark place. Jesus said, 'I am the light of the world. Whoever follows me will never walk in darkness, but will have the light of life' (John 8:12). For me, when I became a Christian, it was as if the light had suddenly been turned on and I could see things for the first time.

Many are fearful of death. One woman said to me that sometimes she couldn't sleep and that she would wake up in a cold sweat, frightened about death, because she didn't know what was going to happen when she died. Jesus said, 'I am the resurrection and the life. Those who believe in me will live, even though they die; and whoever lives and believes in me will never die' (John 11:25–26). Mother Teresa was asked shortly before her death, 'Are you afraid of dying?' She replied, 'How can I be? Dying is going home to God. I've never been afraid. No. On the contrary, I'm really looking forward to it!'

Many people are burdened by worry, anxiety, fear and guilt. Jesus said, 'Come to me, all you who are weary and burdened, and I will give you rest' (Matthew 11:28). Many today are not sure how to live their lives, or whom they should follow. I can remember, before I was a Christian, that I would be impressed by someone and want to be like them, but before long it would be a different person, and then another. Jesus said, 'follow *me*' (Mark 1:17, italics mine).

He said to receive him was to receive God (Matthew 10:40), to welcome him was to welcome God (Mark 9:37) and to have seen him was to have seen God (John 14:9). A child once drew a picture and her mother asked what she was doing. The child said, 'I am drawing a picture of God.' The mother said, 'Don't be silly. You can't draw a picture of God. No one knows what God looks like.' The child replied, 'Well, they will do by the time I have finished!' Jesus said in effect, 'If you want to know what God looks like, look at me.'

Indirect claims

Jesus said a number of things, which, although not direct claims to be God, show that he regarded himself as being in the same position as God, as we will see in the examples that follow.

Jesus' claim to be able to forgive sins is well known. For example, on one occasion he said to a man who was paralysed, 'Son, your sins are forgiven' (Mark 2:5). The reaction of the religious leaders was, 'Why does this man talk like that? He's blaspheming! Who can forgive sins but God alone?' Jesus went on to prove that he did have the authority to forgive sins by healing the paralysed man. This claim to be able to forgive sins is indeed an astonishing claim.

C. S. Lewis puts it well in his book *Mere Christianity*:

> One part of the claim tends to slip past us unnoticed because we have heard it so often that we no longer see what it amounts to. I mean the claim to forgive sins: any sins. Now unless the speaker is God, this is really so preposterous as to be comic. We can all understand how a man forgives offences against himself. You tread on my toes and I forgive you, you steal my money and I forgive you. But what should

we make of a man, himself unrobbed and untrodden on, who announced that he forgave you for treading on other men's toes and stealing other men's money? Asinine fatuity is the kindest description we should give of his conduct. Yet this is what Jesus did. He told people that their sins were forgiven, and never waited to consult all the other people whom their sins had undoubtedly injured. He unhesitatingly behaved as if He was the party chiefly concerned, the person chiefly offended in all offences. This makes sense only if He really was the God whose laws are broken and whose love is wounded in every sin. In the mouth of any speaker who is not God, these words would imply what I can only regard as a silliness and conceit unrivalled by any other character in history.[6]

Another extraordinary claim that Jesus made was that one day he would judge the world (Matthew 25:31–32). He said he would return and 'sit on his throne in heavenly glory' (v. 31). All the nations would be gathered before him. He would pass judgment on them. Some would receive eternal life and an inheritance prepared for them since the creation of the world, but others would suffer the punishment of being separated from him for ever.

Jesus said he would decide what happens to every one of us at the end of time. Not only would he be the Judge, he would also be the criterion of judgment. What happens to us on the day of judgment depends on how we respond to Jesus in this life (Matthew 25:40, 45).

Suppose you saw a man with a megaphone shouting, 'On the day of judgment you will all appear before me and I will decide your eternal destiny. What happens to you will depend on how you've treated me and my followers.' For a mere human being to make such a claim would be preposterous. Here we have another indirect claim to have the identity of Almighty God.

Direct claims

When Jesus was asked, 'Are you the Christ, the Son of the Blessed One?', he replied:

> 'I am... and you will see the Son of Man sitting at the right hand of the Mighty One and coming on the clouds of heaven.' The high priest tore his clothes. 'Why do we need any more witnesses?' he asked. 'You have heard the blasphemy. What do you think?'
> Mark 14:61–64

In this account it appears that Jesus was condemned to death for the assertion he made about himself. A claim tantamount to a claim to be God was blasphemy in Jewish eyes, worthy of death.

On one occasion, when the Jews started to stone Jesus, he asked, 'Why are you stoning me?' They replied that they were stoning him for blasphemy 'because you, a mere man, *claim to be God*' (John 10:33, italics mine). His enemies clearly thought that this was exactly what he was declaring.

When Thomas, one of his disciples, knelt down before Jesus and said, 'My Lord and my God' (John 20:28), Jesus didn't turn to him and say, 'No, no, don't say that; I am not God.' He said, 'Because you have seen me, you have believed; blessed are those who have not seen and yet have believed' (John 20:29). He rebuked Thomas for being so slow to get the point!

If somebody makes claims like these they need to be tested. There are all sorts of people who make all kinds of claims. The mere fact that somebody claims to be someone does not mean that they are right. There are many people, some in psychiatric hospitals, who are deluded. They think they are Napoleon or the Pope, but they are not. So how can we test people's claims?

Jesus claimed to be the unique Son of God – God made flesh. There are three logical possibilities. If the claims were untrue, either he knew they were untrue – in which case he was an imposter, and an evil one at that. That is the first possibility. Or he did not know – in which case he was deluded; indeed, he was insane.

That is the second possibility. The third possibility is that the claims were true.

C. S. Lewis pointed out that: 'A man who was merely a man and said the sort of things Jesus said would not be a great moral teacher.'[7] He would either be insane or else he would be 'the devil of Hell'. 'You must make your choice,' he writes. Either Jesus was, and is, the Son of God or else he was insane or evil but, C. S. Lewis goes on, 'let us not come up with any patronising nonsense about His being a great human teacher. He has not left that open to us. He did not intend to.'[8]

What evidence is there to support what he said?

In order to assess which of these three possibilities is right we need to examine the evidence we have about his life.

His teaching

The teaching of Jesus is widely acknowledged to be the greatest teaching that has ever fallen from human lips. The Sermon on the Mount contains some supremely challenging and radical teaching: 'love your enemies' (Matthew 5:44); 'turn the other cheek' (Matthew 5:39); 'Do to others as you would have them do to you' (Luke 6:31).

John Mortimer, creator of the television series *Rumpole*, explained why, although a long-term atheist, he described himself as 'a leading member of the Atheists for Christ Society'! When asked what brought about this change, he said: 'Seeing the impact on society of a generation that has rejected God and, as a result, Christian ethics. What is beyond doubt is that the Gospels provide a system of ethics to which we must return if we are to avoid social disasters.' The article, which appeared in *The Mail on Sunday* in April 1995, was headed: 'Even the unbelievers should go back to church today.'

Jesus' teaching is the foundation of our entire civilisation in the West. Most of our laws were originally based on his teaching. We are making progress in virtually every field of science and technology. We travel faster and know more, and yet in the past 2,000 years no one has improved on the moral teaching of Jesus Christ.

Bernard Ramm, an American professor of theology, said this about the teachings of Jesus:

> They are read more, quoted more, loved more, believed more, and translated more because they are the greatest words ever spoken... Their greatness lies in the pure lucid spirituality in dealing clearly, definitively, and authoritatively with the greatest problems that throb in the

human breast... No other man's words have the appeal of Jesus' words because no other man can answer these fundamental human questions as Jesus answered them. They are the kind of words and the kind of answers we would expect God to give.[9]

His works

To test the extraordinary claims Jesus made, it makes sense to look not only at what he said but also at what he did. Jesus said that the miracles he performed were in themselves evidence that 'the Father is in me, and I in the Father' (John 10:38).

Jesus must have been the most extraordinary person to have around. Sometimes people say that Christianity is boring. Well, it was not boring being with Jesus.

When he went to a party, he turned water into wine (John 2:1-11). He received one man's picnic and multiplied it so that it could feed thousands (Mark 6:30-44). He had control over the elements and could speak to the wind and the waves and thereby stop a storm (Mark 4:35-41). He carried out the most remarkable healings: opening blind eyes, causing the deaf and dumb to hear and speak and enabling the paralysed to walk again. When he visited a hospital a man who had been an invalid for thirty-eight years was able to pick up his bed and walk (John 5:1-9). He set people free from evil forces which had dominated their lives. On occasion, he even brought those who had died back to life (eg John 11:38–44).

Yet it was not just his miracles that made his work so impressive. It was his love, especially for the loveless (such as lepers and prostitutes), which seemed to motivate all that he did. The supreme demonstration of his love for us was shown on the cross when he laid down his life 'for his friends' (John 15:13). Surely these are not the actions of an evil or deluded man?

His character

The character of Jesus has impressed millions who would not call themselves Christians. For example, Bernard Levin wrote of Jesus: 'Is not the nature of Christ, in the words of the New Testament, enough to pierce to the soul anyone with a soul to be pierced?... he still looms over the world, his message still clear, his pity still infinite, his consolation still effective, his words still full of glory, wisdom and love.'[10] *Time* magazine said this: 'Jesus, the most persistent symbol of purity, selflessness and love in the history of Western humanity.'

Here was someone who exemplified supreme unselfishness but never self-pity; humility but not weakness; joy but never at another's expense; kindness but not indulgence. He was a person in whom even his enemies could find no fault and whose friends said he was without sin. It has been said that our character is truly tested when we are under pressure or in pain. When Jesus was being tortured, he said, 'Father, forgive them, for they do not know what they are doing' (Luke 23:34). Surely no one could suggest that such a man was evil or unbalanced?

His fulfilment of Old Testament prophecy

Jesus fulfilled over 300 prophecies (spoken by different voices over 500 years), including twenty-nine major prophecies fulfilled in a single day – the day he died. Although some of these prophecies may have found fulfilment at one level in the prophet's own day, they found their ultimate fulfilment in Jesus Christ.

I suppose it could be suggested that Jesus was a clever conman who deliberately set out to fulfil these prophecies in order to show that he was the Messiah foretold in the Old Testament.

The problem with that suggestion is, first, that the sheer number of them would have made it extremely difficult. Second, humanly speaking he had no control over many of the events. For example, the exact manner of his death was foretold in the Old Testament (Isaiah 53), the place of his burial and even the place of his birth (Micah 5:2). Suppose Jesus had been a conman wanting to fulfil all these prophecies. It would have been a bit late by the time he discovered the place in which he was supposed to have been born!

His resurrection

The physical resurrection from the dead of Jesus Christ is the cornerstone of Christianity. For me, it was through the life, death and in particular the resurrection of Jesus that I came to believe that there is a God.

The Revd Tom Wright, professor of New Testament and Early Christianity at the University of St Andrews, said this: 'The Christian claim is not that Jesus is to be understood in terms of a God about whom we already know; it is this: the resurrection of Jesus strongly suggests that the world has a Creator, and that that Creator is to be seen in terms of, through the lens of, Jesus.' But what is the evidence that the resurrection really happened? I want to summarise the evidence under four main headings.

1. His absence from the tomb. Many theories have been put forward to explain the fact that Jesus' body was absent from the tomb on the first Easter Day, but none of them is very convincing.

First, it has been suggested that Jesus did not die on the cross, but that he was still alive when he was put in the tomb and that he later recovered. But the physical trauma of a Roman flogging was enough to kill many people. This was graphically brought to life in Mel Gibson's film *The Passion of the Christ*. Jesus was then nailed to a cross and hung upright for six hours. Could a man in this condition push away a stone weighing probably a ton and a half? The soldiers were clearly convinced that he was dead or they would not have taken his body down from the cross. If they had allowed a prisoner to escape, they would have been liable to the death penalty. One New Testament scholar has joked that the only intriguing aspect of this theory is that it keeps coming back from the dead!

Furthermore, when the soldiers discovered that Jesus was already dead, 'one of the soldiers pierced Jesus' side with a spear, bringing a sudden flow of blood and water' (John 19:34). This appears to be the separation of clot and serum which we know today is strong medical evidence that Jesus was dead.[11] John did not write it for that reason; he would not have possessed that knowledge, which makes it even more powerful evidence that Jesus was indeed dead.

Second, some have suggested that the disciples stole the body and began a rumour that Jesus had risen from the dead. Leaving aside the fact that the tomb was guarded, this theory is psychologically improbable. The disciples were depressed and disillusioned at the time of Jesus' death. It would have needed something extraordinary to transform the apostle Peter from a dejected and despondent deserter into the man who preached so powerfully at Pentecost that 3,000 people were converted.

In addition, when one considers how much they had to suffer for what they believed (floggings, torture, and for some even death), it seems inconceivable that they would be prepared to endure all that for something they knew to be untrue.

Third, some have said that the authorities stole the body. This seems the least probable theory of all. If the authorities had stolen the body, why did they not produce it when they were trying to quash the rumour that Jesus had risen from the dead? The authorities (both Jewish and Roman) would certainly have used all the many resources at their disposal to display Jesus' body publicly if they had actually been able to locate it.

Perhaps the most fascinating piece of evidence relating to Jesus' absence from the tomb is John's description of the grave-clothes. In a way, the 'empty tomb' is a misnomer. When Peter and John went to the tomb they saw the grave-clothes, which were, as the Christian author Josh McDowell puts it, 'like the empty chrysalis of a caterpillar's cocoon' – when the butterfly has emerged.[12] It was as if Jesus had simply passed through the grave-clothes. Not surprisingly, John 'saw and believed' (John 20:8).

2. His appearances to the disciples. Were these hallucinations? The *Concise Oxford Dictionary* describes a hallucination as an '... apparent perception of an external object not actually present'. Hallucinations normally occur in highly strung, highly imaginative and very nervous people, or in people who are sick or on drugs. The disciples do not fit into any of these categories. Burly fishermen, tax collectors and sceptics like Thomas are not likely candidates for mass hallucinations! Furthermore, people who hallucinate would be unlikely to suddenly stop doing so. Jesus appeared to his disciples on eleven different occasions over a period of six weeks. The number of occasions and the sudden cessation make the hallucination theory highly improbable.

Furthermore, over 500 people saw the risen Jesus. It is possible for one person to hallucinate. Maybe it is possible for two or three people to share the same hallucination. But is it likely that 500 people would all share the same hallucination? Finally, hallucinating is subjective. There is no objective reality – it is like seeing a ghost. Jesus could be touched, he ate a piece of grilled fish (Luke 24:42–43) and on one occasion he cooked breakfast for the disciples (John 21:1–14). Peter says, '[They] ate and drank with him after he rose from the dead' (Acts 10:41). He held long conversations with them, teaching them many things about the kingdom of God (Acts 1:3).

3. The immediate effect. The fact of Jesus rising from the dead, as one would expect, had a dramatic impact on the world. The church was born and grew at a tremendous rate. As Michael Green, writer of many popular and scholarly works, puts it:

> [The] church… beginning from a handful of uneducated fishermen and tax gatherers, swept across the whole known world in the next three hundred years. It is a perfectly amazing story of peaceful revolution that has no parallel in the history of the world. It came about because Christians were able to say to inquirers: 'Jesus did not only die for you. He is alive! You can meet him and discover for yourself the reality we are talking about!' They did, and joined the church and the church, born from that Easter grave, spread everywhere.[13]

4. Christian experience. Countless millions of people down the ages have experienced the risen Jesus Christ. They consist of people of every colour, race, tribe, continent and nationality. They come from different economic, social and intellectual backgrounds. Millions of Christians all over the world today are experiencing a relationship with the risen Jesus Christ. Over the years I have also experienced that Jesus Christ is alive today. I have experienced his love, his power and the reality of a relationship that convinces me that he really is alive. As the fictional character Sherlock Holmes said, 'When you have eliminated the impossible, whatever remains, however improbable, must be the truth.'[14]

We saw, when we looked earlier in the booklet at what Jesus said about himself, that there were only three realistic possibilities – either he was and is the Son of God, or else deluded or something more sinister. When one looks at the evidence it does not make sense to say that he was insane or evil. The whole weight of his teaching, his works, his character, his fulfilment of Old Testament prophecy and his conquest of death make those suggestions absurd, illogical and unbelievable. On the other hand, they lend the strongest possible support to Jesus' own self-understanding as a man whose identity was God.

In conclusion, as C. S. Lewis pointed out: 'We are faced, then, with a frightening alternative.'[15] Either Jesus was (and is) exactly what he said, or else he was insane or something worse. To C. S. Lewis it seemed clear that he could have been neither insane nor evil, and thus he concludes, 'however strange or terrifying or unlikely it may seem, I have to accept the view that He was and is God.'[16]

Endnotes

1. Josephus, *Antiquities*, XVIII 63f. Even if, as some suggest, the text has been corrupted, nonetheless the evidence of Josephus confirms the historical existence of Jesus.

2. F. F. Bruce, *The New Testament Documents: Are They Reliable?* (Eerdmans, 2003), p.11.

3. F. J. A. Hort, *The New Testament in the Original Greek*, Vol. I (Macmillan, 1956), p.561.

4. Sir Frederic Kenyon, *The Bible and Archaeology* (Harper and Row, 1940).

5. If you are interested in pursuing the subject of Gospel historicity, I would recommend reading N. T. Wright, *Jesus and the Victory of God* (SPCK, 1996) or Craig Blomberg, *The Historical Reliability of the Gospels* (IVP Academic, 2007).

6. C. S. Lewis, *Mere Christianity* (Collins, C. S. Lewis Signature Classics Edition, 2012), pp.51–52.

7. C. S. Lewis, *Mere Christianity* (Collins, C. S. Lewis Signature Classics Edition, 2012), p.52.

8. *Ibid.*

9. Bernard Ramm, *Protestant Christian Evidences* (Moody Press, 1971).

10. By kind permission of Bernard Levin.

11. A team of medical experts produced a detailed study of the physical effects of the treatment which Jesus' body was made to endure based on such circumstantial details and concluded that as a result of hypovolemic shock and exhaustion asphyxia, it would have been a medical impossibility for Jesus to have been alive when he was taken down from the cross (there is a report of the study in *Journal of the American Medical Association*, Vol. 255, 21 March 1986).

12. Josh McDowell, *The Resurrection Factor* (Here's Life Publishers, 1981).

13. Michael Green, *Man Alive!* (IVP, 1968).

14. Sir Arthur Conan Doyle, *The Sign of Four* (Penguin, 2001).
15. C. S. Lewis, *Mere Christianity* (Collins, C. S. Lewis Signature Classics Edition, 2012), p.53.
16. *Ibid.*

Alpha

Alpha is a practical introduction to the Christian faith, initiated by HTB in London and now being run by thousands of churches, of many denominations, throughout the world. If you are interested in finding out more about the Christian faith and would like details of your nearest Alpha, please visit our website:

alpha.org

or contact:
The Alpha Office,
HTB Brompton Road,
London,
SW7 1JA

Tel: 0845 644 7544

Alpha titles available

Why Jesus? A booklet – given to all participants at the start of Alpha. 'The clearest, best illustrated and most challenging short presentation of Jesus that I know.' – Michael Green

Why Christmas? The Christmas version of *Why Jesus?*

Questions of Life Alpha in book form. In fifteen compelling chapters Nicky Gumbel points the way to an authentic Christianity which is exciting and relevant to today's world.

Searching Issues The seven issues most often raised by participants on Alpha, including, suffering, other religions, science and Christianity, and the Trinity.

A Life Worth Living What happens after Alpha? Based on the book of Philippians, this is an invaluable next step for those who have just completed Alpha, and for anyone eager to put their faith on a firm biblical footing.

The Jesus Lifestyle Studies in the Sermon on the Mount showing how Jesus' teaching flies in the face of a modern lifestyle and presents us with a radical alternative.

30 Days Nicky Gumbel selects thirty passages from the Old and New Testament which can be read over thirty days. It is designed for those on Alpha and others who are interested in beginning to explore the Bible.

All titles are by Nicky Gumbel,
who is vicar of Holy Trinity Brompton

About the Author

Nicky Gumbel is the pioneer of Alpha. He read law at Cambridge and theology at Oxford, practised as a barrister and is now vicar of HTB in London. He is the author of many bestselling books about the Christian faith, including *Questions of Life*, *The Jesus Lifestyle*, *Why Jesus?*, *A Life Worth Living*, *Searching Issues* and *30 Days*.